Sussex Money

£10
Savnet

032391
Top

THOMAS DICKER, 1754-1822

Sussex country banker. Born at Buxted. Clerk with Harben & Co., Lewes, 1787-8; clerk, and later a partner in the Lewes Old Bank.

Courtesy of West Sussex County Council Library Service.

Sussex Money

A History of Banking in Sussex

BY

PETER R. JENKINS

Dragonwheel Books

1987

First published 1987 by Dragonwheel Books
Sandcott, Rectory Lane,
Pulborough,
West Sussex,
RH20 2AD

Printed in Great Britain by Consort Print Services, Fareham, Hants.

British Library Cataloguing in Publication Data

Jenkins, Peter R.
Sussex money : a history of banking in Sussex
1. Banks and Banking - England - Sussex - History
I. Title
332.1'09422'5   HG2999.S9

ISBN 1-870177-00-2

Contents

Illustrations

Preface

The industrial history of Britain has received increasing attention in recent years, with the opening of several outstanding museums and the preservation of buildings and other monuments. Great pains have been taken to preserve items of machinery and recreate the working conditions in which they were used. Unfortunately commerce, as opposed to industry, leaves few such relics and yet the industrial revolution of the eighteenth and early nineteenth centuries could not have taken place without an equal revolution in the management of finance and trade. There developed a need for more money in general circulation, for more convenient means of remitting money from one part of the country to another in payment of debts, for raising short-term loans and similarly for depositing relatively small sums at interest without investing directly in a commercial venture. The private country banks prospered by providing these services, familiar enough today, but previously available only in the major cities. However, as trade continued to grow so did the complexity of the banking business and the risks involved, and periodic bank failures became frighteningly common. In 1825, Parliament allowed banks to be financed on the joint stock principle, by many shareholders rather than a few partners, and as a result much larger, stronger organisations developed which eventually absorbed the surviving country banks and amalgamated among themselves to produce the modern high street banks.

The Origins of Banking

All trade, beyond the stage of direct barter, needs either a supply of money or a system of credit. The Romans established both during their occupation of Britain, but it was not until the reign of Offa, King of Mercia between the years 757 and 796 that the first British silver pennies were minted. These penny coins were the basic currency of England for more than five hundred years, being produced by a great many mints using officially approved dies and paying a royalty for the privilege. Prior to the Norman conquest there were about 60 such mints, Sussex being supplied from Steyning, Chichester, Lewes, and Hastings. Coins were also minted at Winchelsea, where the Domesday Book records that a licence fee of 20 shillings per year was payable to the king for the use of dies.

As trade expanded the silver penny was minted in vast quantities and circulated throughout the country in individuals' purses, saddle bags, and even packed into barrels and sacks. When the last of the great castles in Wales was built at Beaumaris, some £6,300 was spent there on food and wages and materials in the year 1295 alone. The whole of this great sum was transported from London and York to Chester and on through north Wales in the form of more than 1,500,000 silver pennies, which were carried by pack horses and protected by writs of safe conduct.[1] To simplify the payment of small sums, which previously had entailed cutting a penny in half, King Edward I introduced the halfpenny and the farthing, while Edward III issued a silver fourpenny groat and a gold coin, the noble, which was worth 6s. 8d. (33p) and intended for use in foreign trade.

Such coinage was the life-blood of common dealing, but large traders, landowners, and the crown had greater needs of finance. The lending of money for interest was forbidden by the Church, so that only those not subject to Church law could carry on such business. Thus it was the Jews who became the moneylenders of Europe, charging rates of interest as high as 40 per cent in view of the great difficulty of ensuring repayment of technically illegal loans. Riots in which Jews were attacked and their records burnt were not uncommonly instigated as a means of avoiding repayment. In England also they were heavily taxed and finally expelled in 1290, when Edward I discovered that merchants from northern Italy could arrange loans despite the Church's rules. The Lombards were particularly skilled in financial matters and acted as collectors of the Papal taxes. Their settlement in London was named Lombard Street and became the centre of banking and finance in the city. The term in 'bank' for a finance house itself derives from the Italian *banco* which was the bench from which a Lombard merchant conducted his business.

In England they combined finance with their general trade, using the Church's tax money to buy English wool which they exported and paying the Pope's revenue out of the proceeds of its sale. Their purchases of wool were often agreed under terms where payment was made in advance for several years' supply, this arrangement often being made with monastries which were effectively given a loan secured against future wool production.

In later years the drovers who brought cattle from the north and particularly from Wales to the markets of London often acted similarly as financial agents. They carried home the proceeds of the sale of their beasts or used the money to settle accounts. They also carried money for that purpose; in 1636 a drover was entrusted with the ship money tax collected in Denbighshire, and a century later one man regularly carried to London sums as large as £400 for Sir Watkin Williams Wynne of Ruabon.[2]

Commercial expansion and a shortage of coin encouraged the use of credit, so that by the eighteenth century many traders found it profitable also to act as a banker, either alone or with partners, making loans, issuing their own bank notes, and redeeming bills of exchange. These were notes signed by an individual or a bank promising to pay a sum of money either on demand or after a certain date, and a healthy profit could be made by discounting the bill, advancing less than the face value on its acceptance and later collecting the full sum. In the north of England bills of exchange signed by trusted men were more highly valued and often circulated more widely than bank notes issued by private bankers. This was not without reason, for the failure of a small bank was all too common and frightening an occurrence.

Banking in the modern sense began in England with the founding of the Bank of England as a means of raising money for King William III in 1694. It was the first joint stock bank, in that it had many shareholders rather than a few partners, and was authorised to raise a share capital of £1,200,000 by the issue of bank notes for public circulation. These were redeemable for gold on demand at the Bank. The entire sum was lent to the government at a rate of 8 per cent interest with an annual charge of £4,000 for managing the loan. The Bank was an immediate success, but a scheme for establishing a land bank soon after was a failure and in consequence a Bank Charter Act was passed in 1708. This forbade any new bank formed by more than six partners to 'borrow, owe, or take up any sum or sums of money on their bills or notes, payable on demand or at a less time than six months from the borrowing thereof'.[3] The Act effectively prevented the growth of any serious competition to the Bank of England by this restriction of note issue, which was long considered the most important and lucrative activity of a bank. There was no such restriction on the private banks, nor on their general trading, but without raising large capital sums by note issue, growth beyond a relatively small local trade was not possible.

In London there grew up many private banks, some descendants of the goldsmiths who had been acting in that role since the time of the Civil War. It had long been accepted practice for them to hold silver and gold plate in their vaults for safe keeping. The receipts given became the earliest form of paper money in England, since they represented solid security against loans or cash advances from the goldsmiths or others. Receipts often changed hands many times before gold was ever claimed. Some of the London banks made note issues, but these were soon stifled by the preeminence of the Bank of England and so they developed solely as financial agents by accepting and lending money and making payments for clients. They were the first to introduce printed cheque forms to replace the handwritten drafts.

Beyond London there traded the many private 'country bankers'. These were the individuals, or more commonly groups of partners less than six in number, who provided financial services within their locality. Note issue provided the capital for the majority of these banks, and as Bank of England notes did not circulate far outside of London and it was not until 1759 that the Bank issued notes as low as £15 and £10 in value (the £5 note did not appear until 1793) the country banks provided a valuable source of credit to an expanding economy. In addition to their local business, country banks maintained an account with one of the London banks and so could remit money to the capital. Similarly a merchant or traveller could provide himself with bills of exchange valid in any parts of the country he wished to visit.

Although there were probably no more than a dozen country banks operating in 1750, by 1797 their numbers had grown to 230 and in 1810 a total of 721 firms was recorded in the Report of the Select Committee on the High Price of Bullion.[4] Such rapid growth was a response to a general rise in business activity and in particular to the increased demand for and dependence on credit that had followed the suspension of cash payments against its notes by the Bank of England in 1797. This had been forced by a financial panic that started on the news of landings of French troops in Pembrokeshire and threatened the national gold reserve as many rushed to exchange notes for gold. It forced a greater reliance on paper money than ever before although the value of a £5 Bank of England note fell to £3 11s. (£3.55) against notes of sound country banks.[5] There was no similar growth in the number of firms in London, their number rising from 69 in 1797 to 73 ten years later, but the London banks did seek urgently to widen their connections with banks in the provinces, and it was at this time that the network of country banks and their London agents was consolidated.

There was little regulation on the working of country banks, no control on the number of notes they might issue, nor on the resources they must maintain to meet their obligations. At a time when the national currency was confused and coin in such short supply that many industrialists and traders were forced to mint their own tokens with which to pay their workers or make change, a country bank was in constant danger of failure from perhaps a single major bad debt. One bank failure could trigger a wave of panic as many customers tried frantically to withdraw their money from other suspect banks which could in turn be brought down. Failure in such a time of panic was the fate of the first banks to be founded in Sussex.

Sussex Banks and Private Tokens

The evidence of the earliest banking activity in Sussex is scanty and uncertain. For many years before commercial banks were established lawyers and merchants had helped their clients to raise loans or place money at interest. As early as 1767, one Richard Peters Rickman of Lewes was described as a 'banker, brewer, and freeholder of the Bear Inn'. The Rickmans were a well-known Quaker family in the town, and there were many Quakers among the early bankers because their reputation for personal integrity was high.

Banking business began to be conducted on a more formal basis in Lewes from the late 1770s by the firm of Thomas Rickman & Son, and from 1782 by one Thomas Harben in partnership with the brothers Thomas and Banister Flight. Harben was a landowner and something of a political schemer who had close connections with the Duke of Newcastle.[6] His interests were wide; in 1782 the Lewes rate book listed him as 'silversmith and banker' while in partnership with the Flight brothers he had considerable dealings in flour and grain.

His Lewes Bank, which came to be known as the Old Bank, operated from Newcastle House in the High Street and conducted the usual business of accepting deposits, making loans and discounting bills of exchange. In 1791 Harben paid £528 2s. 6d. to wine merchants in the City of London on the security of three promissory notes, and gave a mortgage of £120 to 'John Lavender, husbandman, of Warbleton, and John Lavender the younger of St. Leonards, victualler'.[7] Harben had also arranged for the Excise revenue from the eastern part of the county to be paid to the Treasury through his Lewes Old Bank, profitable business for a country banker. For his eldest son Harben obtained the post of Receiver-General of Stamp Duties for Sussex, an office worth £600 per year in the early 1790s and doubtless the monies were remitted through Harben's bank.

In fact by that time Harben was a partner in two other Sussex banks; in 1790 he entered into the partnership of Harben, Shergold, Scott, Rice & Rice to open the Brighton Bank, while he was also a partner with James Lanham and others in the Horsham Bank. In the March of 1793, however, only weeks after the execution of King Louis XVI of France, growing financial instability led to a flurry of bank failures. Six country banks had closed by the end of the month. Two more stopped payment in each of the next three months, three more in July, and another in August. Some of the failures were in the north-west of England and associated with some difficulties in the textile trade; others were in the west, at Bristol, Bath and Worcester, and in Shropshire. On 8 April the *Sussex Weekly Advertiser* reported that 'in the course of the past week, the Lewes Old Bank, the Brighton Bank, and the Horsham Bank all stopt payment; but there is good reason to believe a little time will bring all to rights, and that no material injury will in consequence be sustained'. Harben was himself responsible for many large sums owed as a result of land speculations and on 22 April a meeting of his creditors was held at his house. In May all his estates and other properties were assigned to trustees who were to recover monies owed to Harben and sell such of his assets as would meet his debts.[8] His affairs were settled to the satisfaction of all, for he was a considerable landowner, holding the manors of East Blatchington and Alfriston, with land at Mountfield and Northiam and properties in Lewes and Seaford. It was to Seaford that Harben retired, still taking an active interest in local politics.

From this calamity two of Harben's banks survived; the Horsham Bank was revived under the partnership of Grinsted and Lanham, while the Brighton Bank resumed trading as the Brighton Old Bank run by Messrs. Mitchell, Mills & Co. They failed in 1816 and 1825 respectively. The business of the Lewes Old Bank was taken over by another firm, the Lewes New Bank, to which the clients of Rickman & Son also transferred their accounts during the mid-1790s, when the Rickmans gave up their banking business to concentrate on brewing and other interests.

The New Bank had been founded by four local men, Frances Whitfeld, grocer, Benjamin Comber, gentleman, Richard King, a tallow chandler, and Joseph Molineux, ironmonger, who on 1 July 1789 entered into partnership and each subscribed the sum of £5,000 to the undertaking. Whitfeld has been referred to as a wool dealer, but grocer was his own description although it is probable that he and the others had acted as financial agents for wool dealers and others trading at the Lewes market before establishing the formal banking business.

A trade card preserved at the Lewes branch of Barclays announces that the bank was open from nine in the morning till seven in the evening. It offered interest at the rate of 3 per cent on money deposited for one month, and 4 per cent on deposits made for the term of three months or more. The bank would accept bills of exchange for a discount of 5 per cent of their face value and dealt in Government stock, also offering to collect dividends on behalf of clients. In 1792 Messrs. Comber, Whitfeld, Molineux, and King granted a mortgage of £6,400 to one John Bean against the security of Mays House and farm in Selmeston.[9] The bank survived the storm of 1793 and later began to issue its own notes; despite all successive re-formations of the partnership, there remained members of both the Molineux and Whitfeld families in the firm for more than a century.

Although *The Times* declared in 1793 that 'it is full time that the country should be purged of such nuisances', and wrote of a bubble that had burst, many more banks were being formed. One had been founded at Chichester during the 1780s by Messrs. Ridge and Murray, which became known as the Old Bank on the opening of a rival Chichester and Sussex Bank by Diggins and Co. In 1790 Messrs. Curteis, Curteis, Wollet and Dawes opened the Rye Bank, and there remained a Curteis with the bank throughout its life. The Hastings Bank was founded in 1791, by Messrs. Tilden, Shadwell, Hilder, Harvey and Gill, and its office at 90 High Street proved 'of great utility to the town and especially to the summer visitants, who are now at no loss to get their drafts discounted'.[10] This became known as the Hastings Old Bank when the Hastings, Hailsham, and Ticehurst Union Bank opened as a partnership of Farncombe, Breeds & Co. Soon after this the Brighton Old Bank opened a branch in the town.

Of the men who owned and operated these banks we know comparatively little. One exception is Thomas Dicker of the Lewes Old Bank who died in 1822. His biography, *Memorials of the Life and Times of a late Country Banker*, in fact tells more of his personal life and faith than of his business career, but does record his early years and training. Born in 1754 at Buxted, he went to Uckfield Grammar School then as an apprentice to a local builder, but with the help of a friendly non-conformist minister he sought to further his education. In time a post as clerk was offered by a London banker, but Dicker could not add figures quickly enough.

Instead he obtained a clerkship with a wool merchant on London Bridge, where he remained for three years, later moving to Sheerness until an illness brought him back to Sussex to recuperate at his father's house. In 1780 Dicker became the clerk to Mr Lampert, the Excise Collector for east Sussex. Soon after Lampert was transferred to Kent, taking Dicker to work at Canterbury, where he had some dangerous experiences while pursuing smugglers, and became deeply involved with the work of non-conformist congregations.

His work with the Excise brought him to the notice of Thomas Harben, who invited Dicker to join his Lewes bank when Lampert retired in 1787 though he remained there less than a year, being offered a place in a Canterbury bank by one of his non-conformist friends. A year or two later, however, he returned to Lewes as Harben's chief clerk. He had charge of the daily business of the bank, and when it failed in 1793 Dicker was appointed treasurer to the creditors' trustees. It was suggested that he might become the active partner in a new bank, but politics and finance were unsettled at the time and he declined the offer. In September 1795 he was appointed chief clerk to the Lewes Old Bank of Comber, Whitfeld, Molineux, and King, and in 1807 he became a full partner in the business, still supervising its management until shortly before his death. A man of commercial skill and strong religious faith who had in 1803 been appointed minister of a congregation at Hailsham, Thomas Dicker represented the ideal of a country banker for whom the confidence of the public was his bank's greatest asset. Dicker's son succeeded him as a partner in the Lewes Old Bank in 1823, and he remained with the firm for thirty years until leaving the town.

The growth in commercial activity that had fostered these new private banks brought also an increasingly severe shortage of low denomination coinage. By the 1790s even gold and silver coins were in short supply and no copper pennies, halfpennies, or farthings had been minted for twenty years. The shortage brought particular hardship to the new industrial centres, where employers were forced to pay groups of four or five men with a single note which they in turn were forced to spend together. In 1787 the Parys Mountain Company, which worked the great copper mine of that name on the island of Anglesea in north Wales, began to issue tokens struck from their own metal to pay their workers. These they promised to redeem at the rate of one penny each just as a bank promised to repay the value of its notes, and so began a movement that in time forced the minting of a new national copper coinage.

The ironmaster John Wilkinson soon followed the Parys Mountain Company with an issue of his own, and within a very few months many traders from all parts of the country were ordering these commercial coins, which were produced by the newly mechanised coiners of Birmingham. It could be a profitable business to issue a token, effectively increasing the trader's capital by their value, while offering also some valuable advertising. A new, fashionable hobby developed for the collection of provincial coinage. Tokens bearing no promise of payment were struck and distributed solely for commercial advertisement or political propaganda. Tokens bearing false names from distant places were distributed for fraudulent gain. Nor was it illegal to forge the privately issued tokens, and by 1797 the amount of fraudulent coin in circulation was so great that government was forced to mint new copper penny and twopenny pieces while making the issue of private coinage illegal.

Fewer tokens were issued in Sussex than in industrial districts of the country, but one of the most prolific issuers was Richard Maplesden, a grocer and draper of Winchelsea. In 1794 he had struck two hundredweights of a Winchelsea Halfpenny, so inscribed on the reverse with a representation of the arms of the port of Sandwich, while on the obverse was a bee hive amid overhanging foliage and flying bees surrounded by the legend 'Industry, the source of content'. These tokens were redeemable at his shop in the town. Maplesden also issued a halfpenny token for use at the Brighton Camp of 1794. This was established in response to a French invasion scare, and from August to October 1793 up to ten thousand regular soldiers and militia were kept in readiness at a camp outside Brighton. They were visited by the Prince of Wales.

A second camp was mustered in 1794 with a maximum strength of 15,000 men, and Maplesden's tokens were used in the payment of these troops. Early issues were inscribed as redeemable in Winchelsea, but later coins bore the legend 'Payable in London or Brighton', indicating that Maplesden had established a network of credit similar to that of the banks and their London agents. The tokens themselves showed the bust of a gentleman and the legend 'George, Prince of Wales' on the obverse, with the Prince of Wales' feathers, his motto 'Ich Dien' and the value and date on the reverse. Richard Maplesden almost certainly issued these coins as a profitable venture rather than a loyal gesture. At a third Brighton Camp in 1795 two men were shot and others flogged for mutiny.

Despite the Royal favour of Brighton, the administrative capital of Sussex was Chichester, where several tokens were issued. In 1794 the drapers Dally & Son issued a Chichester Halfpenny bearing a bust of Queen Elizabeth wearing a fine ruff about her neck, and on the reverse a picture of Bishop Story's famous market cross. In the same year Thomas Chaldecott, silversmith

Sussex copper tokens I: Maplesden's Winchelsea Halfpenny, 1794; Dally & Son's Chichester Halfpenny, 1794; Gilbert's Northiam Halfpenny, 1795. 1½ times true size. Courtesy of Worthing Museum.

Sussex copper tokens II: Boorman's East Grinstead Halfpenny, 1795; Battle Halfpenny, 1796; Fisher, Eastbourne, 1796; M. Pintosh, Horsham, 1791. 1½ times true size. Courtesy of Worthing Museum.

and cutler of the town had struck one ton of a halfpenny token payable at his own shop and at that of Thomas Sharp, a mercer, in Portsmouth. This token bore the arms of Portsmouth on the reverse. The arms of the city of Chichester, however, appeared on a token issued at Northiam, near Rye in the east of the county. There James Foller issued a halfpenny 'For the Convenience of Society' as the legend explained. On the reverse were the initials JF as a cypher, with a sheaf of corn above as a symbol of harvest and prosperity. The bee hive similarly represented industry and wealth when it appeared on the Winchelsea Halfpenny, while a token from Lamberhurst was more direct in depicting the harvest of hops under the legend 'May hops for ever flourish'. This was issued by one Thomas Foster, whose family arms appear on the reverse. He was a freeholder and probably a hop grower himself; he certainly appreciated them as the main source of wealth in that area of the Sussex/Kent border country.

Similarly, the Hastings Halfpenny of James Tebay envoked the maritime trade of the town by its depiction of a sloop at sea under sail, while the town arms appear on the reverse. Tebay was an ironmonger and auctioneer, and may have been engaged in shipping himself. James Boorman of East Grinstead was a draper and grocer and indicated such on his halfpenny of 1795 by incorporating a pair of scales in its design above his script initials. He was also a member of the Society of Free Masons, whose arms appear on the obverse, together with the symbols of the carpenter's square and compasses. There were also some non-currency token issues. At Eastbourne, Fisher's Library and Lounge produced in 1796 a medallion in the form of a token which showed the facade of the building and wished 'Prosperity to the Gentry who visit Eastbourne' in the hope that they might in turn visit prosperity on Fisher's Library and Lounge.

By this time fraud had so seriously undermined public faith in tokens that they were outlawed by Act of Parliament in the following year, new coins being minted to take their place. Further issues followed in 1799, 1806, and 1807, but could not keep pace with demand especially as a rise in the price of copper made it profitable to melt for scrap the large coins of 1797 and 1799. By 1810 the metal had started to fall in price and copper mines and smelters were again holding large stocks of unsold metal that could profitably be used to meet the need for small change by producing a 'coinage of convenience'. Once again also there followed the same pattern of over-supply and loss of faith through counterfeiting that combined with a depression in trade to discourage reputable issues after about 1812.

However, a new type of token also made its appearance at this time. An Act of 1809 had required issuers of local tokens to meet claims for the redemption of Bank of England notes, and many new pieces were struck in silver to values of 2/6, one shilling, or 6d. Copper tokens of penny twopenny, or 3d. value reappeared as large, thick coins, while few halfpennies or farthings were struck other than by grocers or tobacconists at a time when half an ounce of tobacco cost 1 3/4d. Public disquiet grew as fast as did the number of tokens in circulation that bore the legends of non-existant backers or were outright counterfeit copies. Petitions were sent to Parliament, one of April 1817 from Dudley claiming that the unredeemable copper coins in use there were exchangeable for no more than half their face value and were no longer necessary. Parliament agreed, passing an Act on 27 July 1817 that prohibited the issue and

Sussex silver tokens. All 1½ times true size. Reproduced by courtesy of Worthing Museum.

circulation of tokens after 1 January 1818; subsequently the government provided adequate supplies of copper coin.

Several remarkable sets of silver tokens were issued in Sussex. J.B. and R. Phillipson were brothers and chemists with shops at Brighton and Chichester respectively; they produced a one shilling token payable at either. At Chichester also, T. Dally & Co. successors to Dally & Son, the drapers who had issued the Chichester Half-penny now produced a Chichester Silver Token valued at 6d. and possibly other denominations. In 1811 the Chichester Accomodation Shilling was issued by a group of four shopkeepers; B. & J. Caffin were drapers in East Street, C. Shipham a grocer in West Street (and the predecessor of Shippam & Co.) while J. Redman was a plumber. That same year Chichester saw the issue of the only recorded complete series of silver tokens valued from 6d. up to a crown piece. These were the Union Tokens, payable at the draper's shops of Henry Comper and Benjamin Charge. A member of the council, Comper was appointed Portreeve, or chief magistrate, on 20 July 1809. He later became a partner in the Chichester Bank. The tokens were actually issued by Benjamin Charge, Jr., a harness maker in East Street and son of the draper. In December 1810 he married Dinah Comper, daughter of the draper, hence the image of the clasped hands and the legend Union Token which appeared on all the coins.

These tokens, like their predecessors of the 1790s eased the shortage of coin, though at the cost of other problems, just as country bankers made available credit. Although by the 1820s the difficulties of national coinage had been mostly resolved, the Bank of England was still far from meeting the demand for circulating bank notes. Thus, with an ever increasing demand for both currency and credit the opportunities were great for enterprising bankers.

Reproduced by courtesy of Worthing Museum.

The Nineteenth Century

The growth in trade that had brought about the shortage of coin was matched by the prosperity of both agriculture and banking while the wars against Napoleon helped to maintain high prices for grain and other produce. Victory at Waterloo and the return of peace brought great changes and a time of danger for bankers. The Horsham Bank run by Charles Grinsted and James Lanham, who had previously been a partner of Thomas Harben, had made large loans to farmers which with its own note issue proved too great a drain of funds; bankruptcy proceedings were held at the George Inn, Henfield, during December 1816. A similar misfortune befell Andrew Burt and his brother John, who became partners in the East Grinstead Bank early in 1807, but much more is known of their business than of others of the period because of papers held at the West Sussex county record office.

John was the active partner and carried on the business from Bank House in East Grinstead High Street, most of his dealings being with farmers and landowners. A banking crisis began in 1814 as the result of too many banks granting too much credit and becoming over-extended. Over the next three years some 89 banks failed. In 1815 the price of wheat collapsed after rising steadily for twenty years and many farmers found it impossible to repay loans. John Burt found it impossible to obtain payment of debts owed to him, and on 28 February 1816 'the East Grinstead Bank stopped payment, a circumstance that will no doubt subject many to inconvenience'. Thus reporting the failure on 4 March, the *Sussex Weekly Advertiser* was 'happy to find . . that no ultimate loss is likely to attend it'. A meeting of creditors was held at the Crown Inn at East Grinstead on 7 March 'at eleven o'clock in the forenoon precisely, to receive a statement of their affairs, and to adopt such measures for an early liquidation of their debts as under the circumstances shall appear most advisable'. A committee of local gentlemen had already examined the bank's accounts and agreed 'that a considerable surplus will remain after repayment of the whole of the demands of the bank'. At the meeting, trustees were appointed on behalf of the creditors to recover the debts owed to the bank, and the Burt brothers were granted time to pay by installments.

At the time of its failure the bank held deposits of £4,010 and had notes in circulation to the value of £11,140. These were its debts, amounting to £15,150, yet the monies owed to the bank totalled £22,089 even after some £11,621 had been deemed irrecoverable.[11] A full list was made of the monies owed to the bank, and this reveals some details of its business. The bulk of the cash had been advanced against the security of bills of exchange and promissory notes, most of them in amounts of between £10 and £100 with some as large as £400 or £500. Other sums included £270 due as a dividend of 4d. in the pound from the bankruptcy of Robert Seppings and an outstanding mortgage of £15,000.

The majority of the customers lived within about ten miles of East Grinstead and by no means all of them were sizable landowners. William Hills of Hartfield was a man of about sixty who was by his own statement 'a poor man who by the earnings of his own labour has brought up a large family' and still in 1817 had seven young children to support. Hills received no support from his parish and expressed himself 'most grateful and thankful to Mr Burt who had the goodness to lend him the sum of £50 to save him from distress and ruin'. He could not repay

East Grinstead Bank. April 6th/1801

Receiv'd of Hastie Esqr

Two hundred Pounds

on acct.

For Messrs. Burt & Co.

£200.. Joseph Barker

Reproduced by courtesy of West Sussex Record Office.

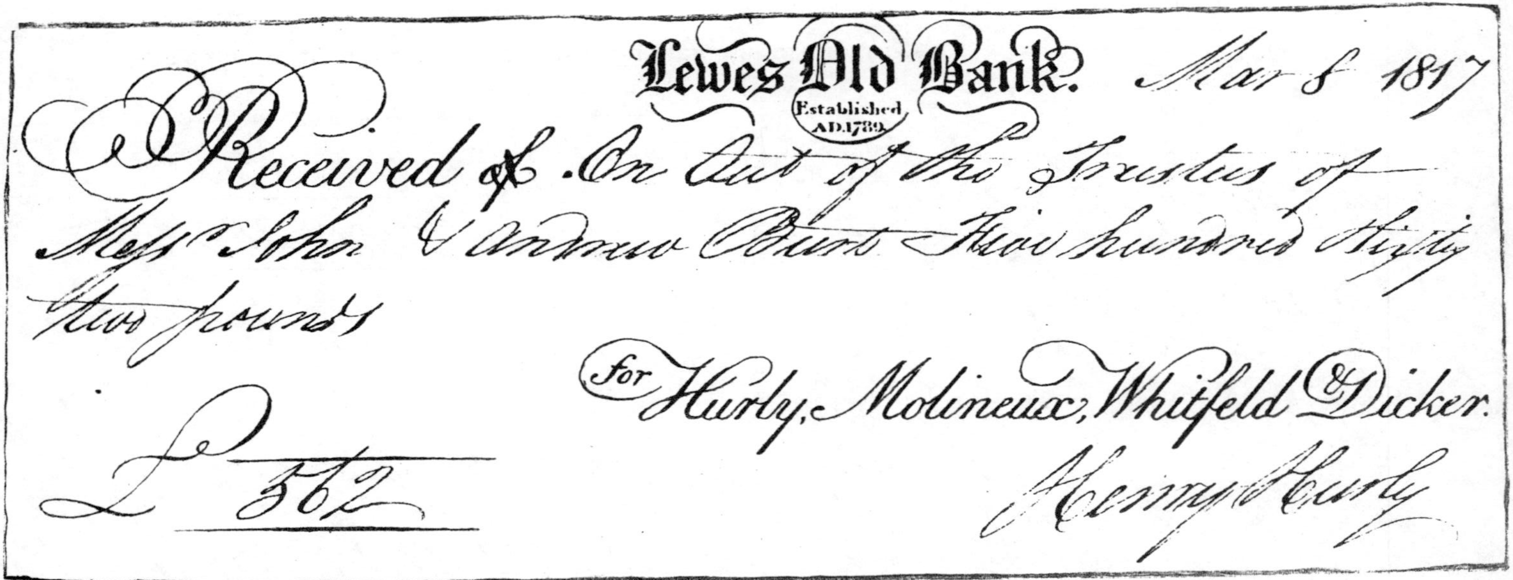

Lewes Old Bank. Established A.D. 1789. Mar 8 1817

Received of Mr. On Acct of the Trustees of Messrs John & Andrew Burt Three hundred sixty two pounds

for Hurly, Molineux, Whitfeld & Dicker.

Henry Hurly

£ 362

Receipt from the Lewes Old Bank for money to be used in settlement of the debts of John and Andrew Burt's bankrupt East Grinstead Bank. The Lewes Old Bank took over the other's business, and this receipt is signed by the Lewes Bank's senior partner. Courtesy of West Sussex Record Office.

this loan, but the parish had agreed to offer the sum of £10 'which they suppose about the value of his goods' toward the settlement of the debt, and this the trustees accepted.[12] The actual collection and distribution of the money was undertaken through the Lewes Old Bank which was by that time a partnership of Messrs Hurly, Molineux, Whitfeld, and Dicker, and although a final settlement was not made for some years, the debts of the East Grinstead Bank were repaid in full.

The lease of the office at Bank House was bought by the Lewes Old Bank in 1818, when an inventory of the fixtures was made which tells something of the character of a country bank of the period.[13] In the banking office was a wide mahogany counter with ink stand and blotter and sets of drawers fitted behind. A cash book would have been kept on the counter in which every transaction was entered. To the rear was an accounting office with a fireplace and two desks where clerks sat on stools. There were two shelves to hold the ledgers and files, and a letter case for correspondence. There were four candlesticks for lighting and brightly polished brass hooks on which to hang hats and coats. Two copper money shovels were provided along with a cash weighing scales. Eight black japanned iron boxes held documents when the bank was trading and a strong box for cash would have been kept in the rear of the office and probably taken down to a strongroom in the cellar at night. The remaining contents of the office were valued at £27 16s. and the premises were let to John Head, solicitor, who also acted as agent for the Lewes Old Bank and effectively provided the services of a branch office. The first true branch of the bank was opened at Tunbridge Wells in 1822.

Since banks served a relatively small area, the opening of branches was the principal means of widening their business. This could either be done directly as in this early instance at East Grinstead, or by the banker joining with some partners in separate but linked ventures in other towns as had Thomas Harben. The banks of the Henty family, the first of which was opened at Worthing in 1809, were built by this latter policy. Born in 1775, Thomas Henty was of an old Sussex family; his ancestors had lived at Antye or Hantye Farm near Wivelsfield as early as the fourteenth century. By the eighteenth century the family had moved to the coast and were farming near Littlehampton. Thomas's father died in 1796 and at the age of 21 Thomas Henty bought a farm of 284 acres at West Tarring for the sum of £12,800.[14]

The farm prospered with the high prices of the Napoleonic period and as his family grew Thomas turned his mind to business. He formed a partnership with his brother George, a Mr. Oliver who was a maternal relative, a Mr. Hopkins who was a nearby landowner and a relation of Henty's wife, and Colonel Margesson, Henty's senior officer in the county yeomanry. Together they founded the Worthing and Sussex Bank at Worthing which was in part financed by an issue of notes in the values of £1, £2, £5, and £10.[15] In the early 1800s a licence to issue notes cost only £30 per year and a stamp duty was payable on each note. Margesson left the bank in 1816 and soon after Edwin Upperton of Thakeham joined the partnership which had opened branches at Horsham and Arundel as separate undertakings with their own note issues. It nevertheless remained very much a family enterprise, with Thomas Henty's eldest son James and later his third son Charles joining him in the business.

Ten years after the final defeat of Napoleon another wave of financial instability broke over the country. Sixty banks failed in England and

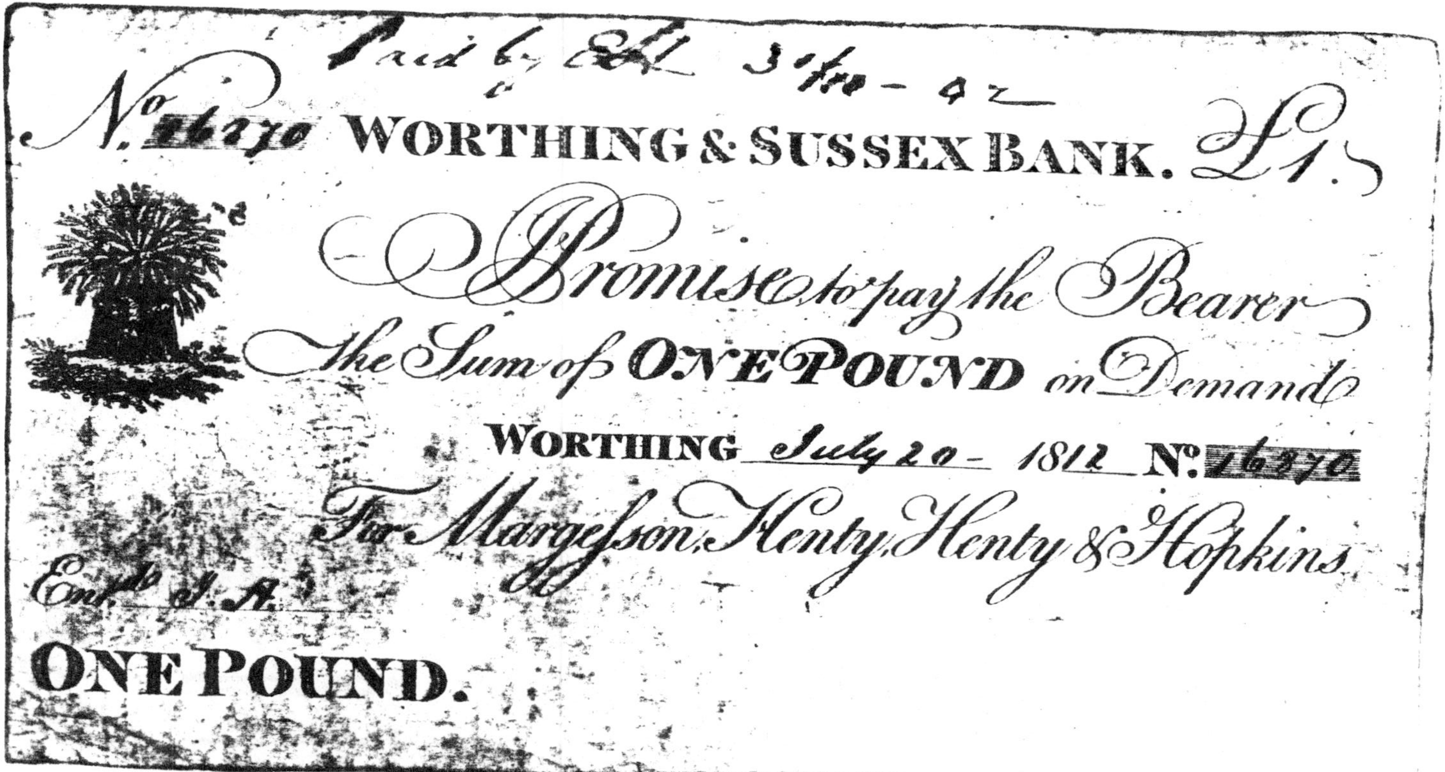

Reproduced by courtesy of West Sussex Record Office.

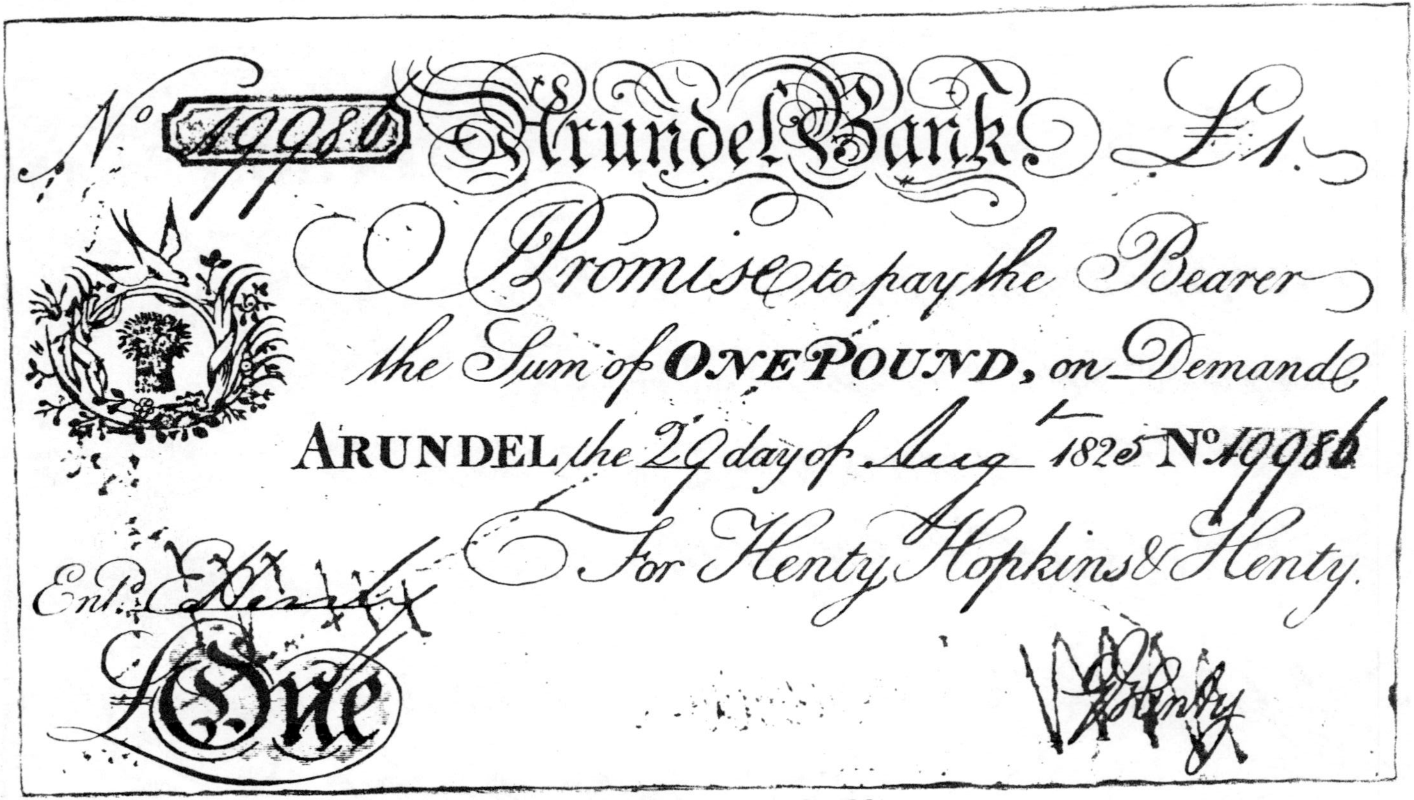

Reproduced by courtesy of West Sussex Record Office.

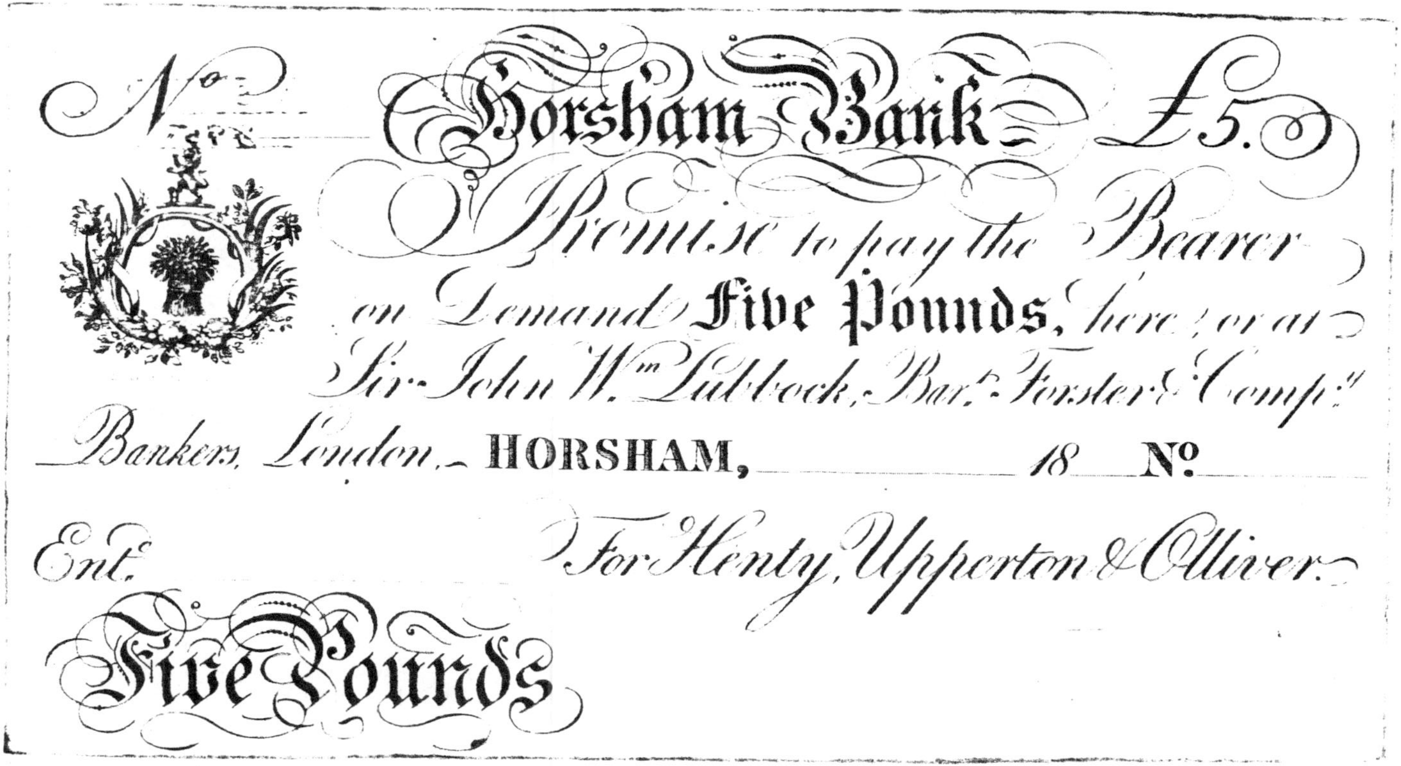

No.

Horsham Bank £5.

Promise to pay the Bearer on Demand Five Pounds, here, or at Sir John Wm. Lubbock, Bart. Forster & Compy. Bankers, London. HORSHAM, 18 No.

For Henty, Upperton & Olliver.

Ent.

Five Pounds

Reproduced by courtesy of West Sussex Record Office.

Sussex was badly affected. The Sussex County Bank of Tamplin & Co. failed at Brighton, as did the Brighton and Sussex Bank run by Lashmar and Muggeridge and the Brighton Old Bank, the last descendant of Harben's banks. The Old Bank had a branch at Hastings, where Messrs. Farncombe, Breeds & Co.'s Hastings & Hailsham Bank also closed. The Lewes Bank of Wood, Hall & Co., established in 1805, was another failure and the crisis almost brought down the Lewes Old Bank.

In December 1825 a rumour spread that the bank was close to failure and many rushed to exchange their notes and withdraw deposits, so bringing closer its failure. To support the bank some 37 local gentlemen and merchants signed and published a declaration on 19 December by which they guaranteed the note issue to the extent of £183,000, mostly in sums of £5,000, though Lord Gage who headed the list stood surity for twice that sum. The printed handbill distributed both in the town and beyond announced that:

> We, the Undersigned, having full Confidence in the Integrity and Responsibility of Messrs Hurly, Molineux, Whitfeld, and Dicker, of the Lewes Old Bank, and wishing to prevent the public and private Evils consequent on the Prevalence of any unfounded Alarm respecting the Safety of their Bank-Notes, do hereby undertake to indemnify the Holders, during the next Six Months, of such Notes to the Amount of the several Sums set against our respective Names.

This had the desired effect, and the firm of Hurly, Molineux, Whitfeld, and Dicker (the son of Thomas Dicker, who had entered the partnership in 1823) emerged stronger for absorbing the business of its erstwhile rival. The means of its salvation met with the full approval of

The Courier, a newspaper frequently critical of country bankers, which observed on 24 December that their:

> safety is literally in their own hands; and if they only remain true to each other, they will have nothing to fear. It is not liberality that they are required to exercise; but simply common prudence. United they may maintain their ground, separated and divided by mutual jealousies or rash confidence in individual strength, their situation must become comparatively hazardous.

In this case the guarantors were also depositors who stood to lose much in the event of a failure but it was nevertheless a bold action. None of the Sussex banks held sufficient cash reserves to stave off a run and they survived through public faith rather than their own soundness. Anecdotes were long after retold of how some had recourse to occasional deceipt, as when 'a crowd of customers were waiting in the bank for their money two clerks with seeming great exertion, would drag to the counter a sack apparently full of sovereigns - which was really full of stones with only a top layer of gold. In this way the waiting customers were led to think that their money was quite safe'.[16]

It was a lean time for bankers, and to worsen matters in 1826 a parcel of bank notes being sent to London by coach from the Worthing bank was stolen. Thomas Henty felt that with some £4,000 of capital invested in the banks and his other businesses producing a very poor return, a better life might be made for his large family in Australia. James, by then manager of the Worthing bank and a merchant in his own right, sailed for New South Wales. In 1828 he wrote to his brother William, who was then twenty years old and a student of law at Lewes, and gave an opinion that despite perhaps looking 'too much on the gloomy side of the question, which has become almost habitual with me from endeavouring to check Father's sanguine calculations upon almost every subject', the family could expect to establish for themselves a sizable farm in the colony. The decision was soon made and in June 1829 three of Henty's sons sailed on the *Caroline*, a ship of 340 tons chartered to carry the livestock and supplies they needed to make a new home ready to receive the rest of the family a year later.

The Hentys soon moved again from New South Wales to Launceston, Tasmania, where James and Charles, who had received his training at the Arundel Bank, continued their involvement with banking. James became a director of the Bank of Australia, and Charles was later appointed its managing director. Thomas Henty devoted most of his time to his first love of farming, building a flock of merino sheep, while also taking an active part in local affairs and acting as chief steward at the races. He died on 25 October 1839 and his death was widely mourned. Many came to the funeral 'notwithstanding the absence of an invitation to attend'. The *Launceston Advertiser* reported that the coffin was followed by 'a vast train - comprising all the leading settlers this side of the colony - the military and civil officers - and the tradesmen of the town; all equally anxious to manifest their respect for the memory of the deceased, and the family of which he was the revered head . . Too nobly proud to associate himself with the petty party differences he lived a faithful sample of the English Country Gentleman'.[17]

The banks he had founded in Sussex were all carried on by partnerships dominated by other Hentys, nephews and descendants of the founder.

Other, new banks grew up alongside them, and by chance the founders of one also had some family connections with Australian pioneers. By 1809 there were already two banks operating in the city, the Chichester and Sussex Bank of Messrs Diggins & Co., of whose business little is known but the name, and the Chichester Old Bank under the management of William and Charles Ridge and Richard Murray. The Old Bank made a note issue, and it was for forging a £5 note of the bank that John Binstead was hanged at Newgate in 1815. Binstead was a drawing teacher and he had forged the note by hand using a camel hair brush and Indian ink. On the scaffold he asked of the chaplain in attendance that his hands 'might not be applied to persons who came to be rubbed for the wen' it being a common belief that the touch of a hanged man could relieve the swelling of warts and other skin ailments. Whether this wish was respected is not known, but the forged note that had brought Binstead to the scaffold still survives in the care of the West Sussex county record office.[18]

The new bank opened at 74 East Street on 13 November 1809 as the result of a partnership between James and William Hack, Charles Dendy, and James Farenden, who each subscribed £2,500. The Hacks were brothers and the eldest of ten children of James Hack, a Quaker who had moved from Basingstoke in 1755 to establish himself in Chichester as a maker of pattens, wooden-soled clogs or overshoes with leather uppers. He came from a family employed in the leather trade, and also a family that had been one of the earliest members of the Society of Friends in Hampshire. James and William were born a few years after the move, in 1758 and 1759 respectively, and both went into trade as merchants in Chichester. The brothers were dissimilar in character, as James Hack's granddaughter, Maria Taylor, many years later recalled, for William's face 'was so full of dreamy thoughts as he sat by my comely, well satisfied grandfather . . he was clever, quite witty, perhaps rather sarchastic, while my grandfather knew nothing of humour . . (William) had good taste and always made excellent wedding presents'.[19] A third brother, Stephen Hack, followed their father into the leather trade with a business in Little London. He was the father of ten children, two of whom, James and Stephen, emigrated to become pioneer settlers in what is now South Australia. Charles Dendy was also a leather merchant and glover who traded in Chichester, while James Farenden was a timber and coal merchant and general dealer. Their bank was thus founded on the profits of trade, as had been the Lewes Old Bank.

Of the £10,000 subscribed by the partners, £1,200 was paid to Farenden for the premises in East Street, beneath which was a complex of cellars suitable for use as a strongroom. About £100 was spent on items of furniture and general equipment, including an iron chest bought from William Ridge of the Chichester Old Bank. The sum of £3,000 was deposited with Masterman & Co. who were to act as the bank's London agents, and on the first day of business three accounts were opened; one Richard Doone deposited £100, while Robert Bass of Brighton borrowed £200 and Juliet Cooke borrowed £35 against promissory notes. The bank was successful, for some years paying a dividend of five per cent per annum to the partners, but it confined its dealings to the area around Chichester. Although an agreement was made in 1810 with Peter Martin, surgeon, and James Jacob, grocer, for them to act as agents of the bank at Pulborough, nothing came of the idea and the Chichester Bank never opened any branches.[20]

Another bank that confined itself for many years to its home town was that established in 1805 by Thomas Browne, Nathanial Hall, Richard Lashmar, and Thomas West as the Brighton Union Bank. Offices were opened at 6, 7, and 8 North Street on 1 August, and the first customer was Daniel Constable, a draper whose shop was at 3 North Street. The partnership was formed with a capital of only £1,500, and to compensate for this a large issue of notes was placed in circulation. These were in values of £1, £2, £5, five guineas, and £10, and arrangements were made for them to be distributed by Bushby's Bank of Arundel, a small bank absorbed by Henty & Co. when their Arundel Bank was opened a few years later, and by a Mr. Turner who became an agent for the Brighton Union Bank at East Hoathley and Seaford.

To further encourage the use of their notes Thomas West wrote to the Customs and Excise Department, guaranteeing the worth of the notes if accepted for payment of duties; Government departments had often been the losers when banks failed. These efforts succeeded in widening the circulation of notes, but at some cost. By the end of 1805 notes to the value of £41,275 had been issued, but over £400 paid out for their printing. Some of the money raised by the issue and accepted as deposits was invested in Government securities; £4,000 in 3 per cent Annuities and £6,880 in India Stock. Nevertheless, after three months' trading the bank showed a surplus of only £4 19s. when it had opened 70 accounts. The number grew to about 350 by 1820, but none were very large. There was no real return to the partners for some years, and there were further difficulties to come.

In 1807 the firm of James Tamplin, Creasy & Gregory opened for business in Brighton as the Sussex County Bank, and in 1818 Richard Lashmar left the Union Bank to open the Brighton and Sussex Bank under the partnership of Lashmar and Muggeridge. Far worse, on Wednesday 5 February 1812 the Union Bank was the victim of a bold robbery. A parcel of bank notes of £1, £5, £10, £30, and £50 denominations totalling £3,031 in value, was being returned from Messrs. Weston, Pinhorn & Co.'s Borough Bank, London agents of the Union Bank. The notes were packed in a box which was locked inside the coachman's box of the Blue Coach, which ran daily to and from London. On arrival the coachman's box was found to be unlocked and the case of notes missing. Suspicion fell at once on the group of young men who had taken all four seats inside the coach. They were apparently 'known to the Bow Street officers', but none of them were traced.

On 17 February, the *Sussex Weekly Advertiser* commented that 'a more systematic robbery was perhaps never committed' since it was thought that one of the party had picked the lock of the driver's box while the coach was stopped at an inn, probably while the others kept watch or diverted the coachman's attention. The newspaper added a hope that 'the perpetrators will be disappointed in their golden expectations by the difficulty of negotiation, as the numbers of the notes were all known and the payment of them stopped'. The numbers were advertised in the press, together with the offer of a reward by the London bank of one hundred guineas for any information leading to the conviction of the thieves. They offered a further reward of ten per cent of the value of any notes recovered, while the Brighton Union Bank, 'the more effectually to prevent the circulation of their stolen notes' issued a new series of notes printed from a plate 'that renders them perfectly distinguishable' from those of the type stolen, and the old notes cancelled as soon as the bank received them.

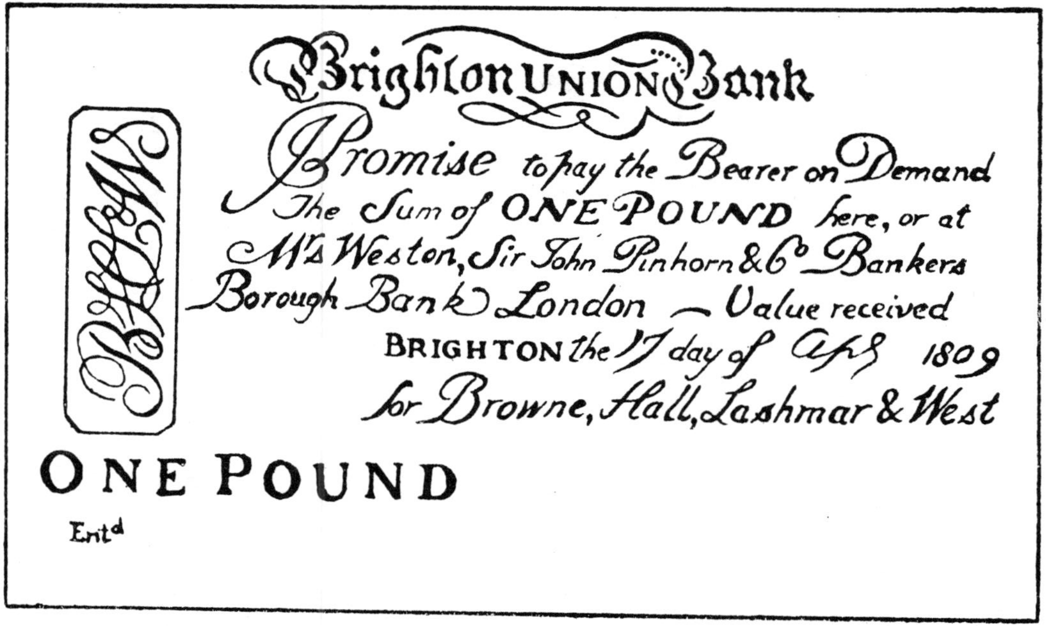

One of the Brighton Union Bank notes stolen in the Blue Coach robbery of 1812. The bank warned against accepting notes of this type dated prior to 1812, but the thieves managed to spend many of them which the bank had to honour. Reproduced by courtesy of Barclays Bank PLC.

Reward & Caution.

100 GUINEAS REWARD

WILL BE PAID BY

MESSRS. BROWNE, HALL, & CO.

OF THE

Brighton Union Bank,

FOR THE

APPREHENSION AND CONVICTION

OF

One or more of the Persons,

CONCERNED IN THE

ROBBERY

OF

THE UNION BANK NOTES

OUT OF THE

BLUE COACH,

On the Fifth of FEBRUARY last.

MESSRS. BROWN, HALL, and CO.

Beg to *caution* all Persons from receiving in payment *any* of the NOTES of the

OLD IMPRESSION,

Which are particularly distinguished,

By their being *all* dated *prior* to the present Year, 1812:—

And further distinguished,

BY BEING TOTALLY DIFFERENT

From the Notes of the New Impression,

BROWNE and CO. are now issuing.

FLEET, PRINTER, BRIGHTON.

Reproduced by courtesy of Barclays Bank PLC.

Nothing was heard for a month, until on 23 March the *Advertiser* announced that 'a few days since a man named Burkitt was taken up . . charged with uttering, at Maidstone in Kent, two of the fifty-pound notes of the Brighton Union Bank that were stolen from the Blue Coach'. He was to be examined by magistrates that day, and the paper hoped that 'it will lead to a full disclosure of the feloneous transaction, and that the perpetrators of it may in consequence be brought to condign punishment'. It was thus with regret that the *Advertiser* had to report two weeks later that Burkitt had 'contrived to make his escape from the officers who had him in custody prior to his examination'. He was not recaptured, and the stolen notes were still appearing in circulation despite the efforts of the Brighton Union Bank to speed the exchange of its old notes for new. By 1 June the bank had several times advertised the numbers of the stolen notes and further 'having evidence that some persons concerned in the robbery are taking opportunities to pass the stolen notes by altering their numbers, and by other nefarious artifices', they warned the public against accepting any notes of the old impression. To what extent the thieves ultimately profitted from their crime will never be known, but notes with a value of more than £300 were successfully exchanged and paid when returned to the bank and nobody was ever brought to justice. The loss to the bank was great, especially when coupled to the cost of printing new notes and almost forced it into failure.

Two years after this robbery a second bank was established at Brighton by William Wigney, a draper from the north of England who had opened a shop in North Street. In 1814 he opened the Brighton New Bank or the Brighthelmston Bank as a family undertaking with an office in East

Street. The bank issued notes, and at the Lewes Assizes of July 1815 William Wigney brought a prosecution for libel against one John Howell, alleging that Howell had written comments on 'certain bank notes of the Brighton New Bank, reflecting upon the character and conduct of Mr Wigney'.[21] In the event Wigney withdrew his evidence before the case came to trial and a verdict of not guilty was recorded.

The Wigneys 'became magnates in the society of Brighton' and of William's four sons one founded the Kemp Town Brewery and the eldest, Isaac, 'a man of dash and enterprise' was a magistrate and Member of Parliament for Brighton where he was a leader of local society. Their bank thus attracted many of the better accounts, including that of Hannington's, successors to Daniel Constable, first customer of the Union Bank, and the Corporation of the town. In 1841 Isaac was again returned as M.P. after a gap of some years and in that year 'reached the zenith of power and social distinction'.[22] Soon after he was the central figure in one of the two sensational bank failures that shook Sussex in a period of four months.

Bankruptcy and Scandal

In November 1841 the Chichester Old Bank failed suddenly in circumstances that led to criminal as well as bankruptcy proceedings. The bank was by then a partnership of brothers William and Charles Ridge with William Newland. Charles was the senior partner; he received the whole of the profits of the bank while his brother was paid £800 and Newland £600 per year. In comparison, William Williams, the bank's chief clerk, had an annual salary of £130. On Saturday 13 November the bank closed in the evening as usual. It did not open again.

The news caused panic in the city, partly at least because the funds of several charities had been on deposit, including about £1,000 of the Chichester Infirmary's funds. The partners, with their principal cashier, William Styles Goodeve, who had been with the bank for thirty years though he had latterly also traded as a merchant on his own account, and William Williams who had been employed for a similar length of time since leaving school, began the task of totalling the debts and assets of the bank. This was no simple matter, for accounts were kept on a daily basis by totalling transactions without counting the notes and cash actually held. A cash book was kept on the counter in which clerks entered all payments and deposits. This book was balanced by one of the cashiers or by Newland, and each evening each of the clerks made out a 'telling-up' paper recording the amount of cash he had returned from his drawer at the counter to the strongroom in the cellars. These figures were entered in a telling-up book, but there was no independent check on the cash in the strongroom.

As principal cashier, Goodeve was responsible for most of the accounting and although the partners looked at the cash book, they did not regularly check its accuracy. He had custody of one of the keys to the strongroom, the iron door of which was fitted with two locks. Goodeve and Williams each held a key to one of the locks, while the partners held the keys to the other. There was also a mechanical puzzle lock which needed no key. Goodeve had charge of the bank's note issue. He brought further supplies of notes from a box in the strongroom as required by the clerks and kept records of the numbers in circulation to make up the annual return for the Treasury. On Saturdays a list was made of the notes held of the Petersfield, Arundel, and the other Chichester bank. These in turn told the Chichester Old Bank which notes of theirs had been accepted. Once so notified the banks deemed them cancelled and arranged for their return.

On 17 November William Newland asked Goodeve for the total value of notes in circulation; he 'went into the front office and produced a paper on which was £8,685'. Newland then asked 'what he had got to provide for it; when he replied about £400 worth of hay and other things'. As the accounting continued it became clear that there was considerable deficiency in the bank's funds, greater even than that which had caused the suspension of payments. By Friday 19th, it was clear that while on paper there appeared to be in Goodeve's custody some £1,549 2s. 10d. in cash and £35,000 in notes of the bank, there was in the cellars only about £400 in cash and some £16,000 in notes. The partners knew of shortage of £11,500, but were shocked to find £5,050 more to be missing from Goodeve's account and £1,749 12s. 4d. from Williams' separate account. Both admitted that their figures were 'altogether fictitious' and Williams said he had first taken money 'twelve or thirteen years ago, when some of his family were in distress' but had taken none for several years. Both were cautioned and they declined to say anything further. They were brought before the magistrates on 26 November and charged with embezzlement. Bail was refused and their trial set for Monday 3 January 1842.

By December the *Sussex Agricultural Express* was 'much pleased to find that confidence is in great measure restored in this city. Energetic measures were undertaken by the inhabitants to meet the temporary inconveniences to which they were subjected, and as the surplus funds of several charities were locked up . . the public immediately stepped forward and furnished, to a great extent, the necessary means for the occasion'. Bankruptcy proceedings were begun against the partners and it was announced that a meeting of creditors would be held on Monday 20 December at the Dolphin Inn to choose trustees to supervise liquidation of the bank's assets. The *Express* reported that 'a strong contest is expected as the parties have been canvassing for a fortnight and it seems to excite as much interest as an election. It is the West Street against the Pallant'. At that meeting a compromise was reached and creditors proved debts totalling £115,475 11s. 1d.

The trials of Goodeve and Williams aroused even more excitement and 'from an early hour every avenue leading to the Town Hall was crowded'. Proceedings began at ten o'clock, when Williams was brought into the dock on the charge of embezzling cash; he was charged separately with taking notes of the bank, as was Goodeve. Williams 'was respectably attired, and appeared about 50 years of age, and pleaded to the indictment in a firm voice "not guilty".' The prosecution called Charles Ridge and William Newland as witnesses to explain the accounting methods that had allowed the deficiencies to remain concealed for so long and how they had at last come to light. Speaking for the defence 'Mr Chambers rose and addressed the jury at considerable length for the prisoner, and then called a number of highly respectable witnesses who gave the prisoner an excellent character. After which the learned Recorder summoned up at considerable length, explaining the law, and afterwards reading the evidence and commenting on it as he proceeded. The jury retired at a quarter before eight, and, after an absence of a quarter of an hour, returned a verdict of not guilty. The announcement was followed by shouts of applause'. Since there was no more evidence to offer on the charge of embezzling bank notes, or in the case of Goodeve, verdicts of not guilty were recorded on those charges also. The trial had lasted nearly ten hours and the wide popularity of the outcome reflected a general feeling that it was the partners of the bank, and the Ridge brothers in particular, who were responsible for its failure.

Bankruptcy proceedings resumed at the Dolphin Inn on Friday 14 January, when a further £7,121 4s. 10d. of debts were proven, bringing the total to £122,646, and the examination of the partners and their accounts began. Charles Ridge appeared first and 'underwent a long examination upon the state of their business affairs before 1830, which terminated without eliciting any fact of importance to the creditors'. On Tuesday 15 February William Goodeve was declared bankrupt, and on Wednesday William Newland underwent his examination at the Dolphin. 'It did not occupy more than an hour, when Mr John Sherwood, on behalf of the creditors, expressed his satisfaction at the manner in which he had conducted himself'. The examination of Charles Ridge was resumed on Thursday and proceedings continued on

Courtesy of West Sussex Record Office.

Souveniers of two great scandals. Above: a note of the Chichester Old Bank which was exhibited at the bankruptcy hearings. Signed by William Ridge and entered in the account book on issue by William Newland. Below: a £10 note of the Brighthelmston Bank signed by Isaac Wigney.

THE WAY THINGS GET ABOUT.

Young Smith. "THEY SAY THE MIDDLESEX AND JERUSALEM BANK HAS SMASHED."

Old Brown. "BOSH! I HAPPEN TO KNOW THE CONTRARY."

Young Smith. "REALLY? THEN IT MUST BE THE MIDDLESEX AND SOMETHING ELSE; BUT I DO THINK THERE SHOULD BE SOME WAY OF *PUNISHING* THE IDIOTS WHO GO SPREADING THESE REPORTS ABOUT."

Banks could be gravely harmed, even forced into failure, by the spread of a rumour of weakness. Reproduced by permission of *Punch*.

Friday and Saturday although 'the investigation was not of the satisfactory character which the creditors expected'. It took many more weeks to resolve the tangled affairs of the Chichester Old Bank, and ultimately it paid no more than 1s. 4d. in the pound of its debts. But by then another and greater scandal had broken with the failure of the Brighthelmston Bank.[23]

William Wigney, the bank's founder, had died in 1836 and the Brighthelmston Bank was never again solvent. Its troubles stemmed largely from the business dealings of Isaac Newton Wigney, M.P., who became chief partner with his brother Clement on their father's death. During 1841 Isaac had invested more than £8,000 in a London factory that made sugar from potato flour; he had received only £700 in return. It was not the first and not the greatest of his dubious ventures. In 1836 he had advanced £6,722 to a factory producing India rubber belts, but the bank's greatest losses were sustained through involvement with a Glasgow enterprise. As Isaac Wigney himself explained:

> In the beginning of the year 1833, being in Parliament, I was introduced to Captain Charles Stuart Cochrane, R.N., son of the late Admiral Sir Thomas Cochrane, R.N., and was afterwards referred by him to his brother in law, Captain Thomas Troutbridge, Bart., R.N. and M.P., and to Admiral Sir Philip Durham, R.N., M.P., etc., who not only spoke of him in the warmest terms, but gave him the highest character for honour, integrity, etc. These circumstances induced me to listen to a proposition from Captain Cochrane to join him in carrying out the manufacture of merino wool-spinning in Glasgow, on a principle never before known or acted upon in this country, and which had received the sanction

> and authority, with two premiums of £300 each of the Board of Trustees for the Encouragement of the Arts and Sciences of Scotland. Consequently, after making the most anxious inquiries from merchants and manufacturers, from whom I obtained the most favourable opinions as to the outcome of the project . . Captain Cochrane immediately went down to Glasgow and laid the foundations of that ruin to me and my family.[24]

Wigney advanced more than £30,000 from the bank to support this venture and the cash disappeared entirely, while the *Sussex Agricultural Express* commented that 'the concern at Glasgow is likely to turn out a very sorry affair for the creditors. Mr Wigney appears to have been completely fleeced by the wily Scotch'. Fleeced quite as thoroughly, in fact, as any merino sheep.

Rumours about his bank's finance caused some tradesmen to withdraw their accounts during February of 1842. Wigney was still paying money to the Glasgow business so that 'the bank was drained to the utmost' and 'so lately as the 2nd or 3rd of the present month (March) a sum of £2,000 was paid by Masterman & Co.', the London agents. On Friday 4 March a notice was posted on the door of the bank announcing that 'Messrs Wigney & Co. deeply regret the painful necessity of suspending their payments'.

Bankruptcy proceedings followed against both Isaac and Clement Wigney, and on Friday 22 April the public examination of Isaac began in the Town Hall at Brighton. Matters began with a probing of the investments he had made using the bank's money and when Wigney proved increasingly vague or unable to answer, the criticism became sharper, especially when Wigney admitted he had known the bank to be insolvent since the death of his father. Previously the bank had been secured by William's personal assets which were valued at nearly £100,000. On his death the estate had been divided, and only by leaving a part of the sum on deposit on behalf of the beneficiaries could the bank continue to trade. Isaac had hoped to recover his own fortunes and those of his bank by means of his investments. He had only succeeded in greatly worsening the position and it was the presentation for payment of bills of exchange drawn against the Brighthelmston Bank that should have been accepted and paid by the Glasgow business that precipitated the failure of the bank, which 'paid until it could pay no longer'.[25]

These admissions brought widespread anger from the creditors, but that was as nothing compared to the scandal that followed from accusations that Isaac Wigney had removed and hidden much valuable property from his house in Adelaide Terrace after being declared bankrupt. Parcels of silver plate and glassware were found at the brewery owned by Isaac's brother George and Wigney's London house and that of his mother in-law, and at Brighton railway station. Some servants at the Adelaide Terrace house were questioned, and Wigney disclaimed all knowledge of the affair, saying he had only arranged for a few trunks of clothes to be packed. Mr Bennett, appearing for the creditors, declared that 'he believed the conduct of the servants and the bankers had been alike disgraceful'. Wigney's affairs and those of the bank were in a very bad state, with debts amounting to more than £120,000, and the *Sussex Agricultural Express* was correct in observing that 'the concern will produce little or nothing for the creditors. In short, so bad a business as this we have scarcely heard of'.[26]

Arms of the Westminster Bank, founded in 1834 as the London and Westminster, the first joint stock bank in the capital, and a monogram of the National Provincial Bank of England, (NPBE), which amalgamated as the National Westminster Bank.

The Joint Stocks

Such failures as these were not uncommon in the early 1840s, which was a period of instability in country banking as had been the years 1815-16 and 1825-26. Between 1825 and 1842 the number of private country banks fell from 554 to 331; this was not simply due to weaknesses of finance or management, but reflected also the rise of joint stock banking in England.

In 1825 there began a financial crisis which led to the failure of 93 banks; Sussex was badly affected, with six banks closing. The crisis prompted Parliament to remove the restriction of 1708 that had effectively limited the number of shareholders in a bank to six. In Scotland the banks had suffered from no such restriction and had proved both more stable and more prosperous, though by no means free from failures. Therefore an 'Act for the better regulation of Co-Partnerships of certain Banks in England' was passed in May 1826, and permitted the formation of banking partnerships having any number of shareholders, and the right to issue notes provided they did not operate within a radius of 65 miles of the capital. This area was to remain the preserve of the Bank of England and included the whole of the county of Sussex. The first true provincial joint stock bank was opened in Lancaster in 1826 and by the end of 1833 there were nearly fifty trading in England with a total of nearly 10,000 shareholders.[27]

These offered no competition to the private banks of Sussex, being protected by the Bank of England's monopoly. In 1832, however, it was suggested that joint stock banks might even be established in London provided that they made no issue of notes, which few London banks did in view of the overwhelming position of the Bank of

England. This opinion was upheld after study of the Bank's charter, and a clause permitting the formation of such banks was inserted in an Act of 1833 when the charter fell due for renewal. A joint stock bank was formed quickly by a group of Scotsmen and with an office in Throgmorten Street and another in Waterloo Place it was named the London and Westminster Bank. The great novelty of these banks lay in providing 'an impersonal banking service, financed by many small proprietors, and relying on the facilities it could place at its clients' disposal. That there was a need for something of the sort is proved by the rapidity with which the idea was taken up'.[28]

By 1842 there were 118 joint stock banks operating in England with five in London which included the National Provincial Bank of England and the London and County Bank. The latter was founded in 1836 as the Surrey, Kent and Sussex Joint Stock Bank, changing its name three years later to emphasise its connection with the money markets of London and its expanding area of operation. In 1839 the bank had three branches in Sussex, at Brighton, Horsham, and Lewes. At the time there were some twenty offices or branches of banks in the county.

The Henty banks established a fourth office at Steyning which was opened on only three days of the week, being manned by a clerk from the Horsham Bank. This was robbed in 1840, when two men hid in the building and took the keys of the strongroom from beneath the manager's pillow as he slept; it was common for the manager and even some of the clerks to live above the office of a bank. The thieves removed £450 from the strongroom, then helped themselves to food and drink before making good their escape.

Both the Chichester Old Bank and its newer rival were still in business, as were both the

Brighton Union and Brighthelmston banks. William and John Stoveld ran a small banking office at Petworth, while Messrs. Hopkins and Drewitt operated banks in both Petworth and Arundel. The Petersfield Bank and opened a branch at Midhurst while in the east of the county Messrs. Curteis, Pomfret & Co. had a bank at Rye. The Hastings Old Bank operated seven branches, three of them at Hastings, St. Leonards, and Battle, with four more over the border in Kent. Although still in their infancy, the joint stock banks were soon to bring Thomas Henty's fears for the future of the private banks nearer to fruition. As he had recognised, the heyday of the country banks had passed, and the next half century was to see both general expansion of banking services with much increased competition between these local private banks and the joint stocks.

The Lewes Old Bank maintained its branch at Tunbridge Wells, while the East Grinstead agency had passed from John Head to his son George, who was also a solicitor. In 1842, shortly after the failures of the Brighthelmston and Chichester Old banks, George Head established a business of his own called the East Grinstead Bank, as had been that of John and Andrew Burt some thirty years before, but the future of banking in the county lay with an expansion of the existing banks rather than the founding of new ones. One John Smith was appointed agent for the Lewes Old Bank at East Grinstead; he was succeeded by Mr. William Rudge, upon whose death in 1887 the bank took over direct management. New offices were opened at Eastbourne, Seaford, Newhaven, and Uckfield, where the bank's business had before been conducted by an agent from his shop. By 1891 the assets of the Lewes Old Bank exceeded one million pounds, of which £100,000 represented the partners' capital. Henty & Co. opened a fifth branch office at Littlehampton, while at

Brighton the Union Bank was the sole beneficiary from the failure of the Wigneys' Brighthelmston Bank, recovering some of the more profitable business of the town. After its various early difficulties the bank was set on a course of steady prosperity; it opened branches at Hove and at Cuckfield, and later at Burgess Hill and Haywards Heath. At the same time, the Hampshire Banking Company moved into Sussex with branches at Brighton and Chichester.

By contrast, at Hastings 'the townspeople were thunderstruck' when on 26 June 1857 the Old Bank of Messrs Hilder, Smith, and Scrivens closed its doors and suspended payments. The *Hastings and St. Leonards News* observed that 'in the first feeling of vague surprise and alarm, the idea most prevalent seemed to be that complete and irretrievable ruin had overtaken us all. As men's minds got to look at the melancholy affair in a steadier and cooler way, some rays of hope appeared through the fearful gloom that, for the moment, had settled on the general mind with so great an intensity and with so much of hopeless horror'. Such shock was common on hearing the news of a bank failure, but in this case it proved not wholly justified. The immediate cause of the failure had been the sudden bankruptcy of one Richard Smith, a farmer at Salehurst who was related to two of the partners and to whom the bank had lent a large sum. The Hastings Old Bank had debts exceeding £150,000, but there were considerable assets and payment at the rate of 13s. 3d. in the pound was quickly promised.

To help those in difficulties until a settlement was made, a group of local men raised a subscription by advancing money against notes of the bank held by creditors. This relieved much immediate distress since bankruptcy proceedings against the partners were delayed because 'James

Hilder, an old man of 86 who had been manager of the Robertsbridge branch, proved unexpectedly obstructive. One of his ledgers was destroyed, and his examination had to be repeatedly deferred'. Tilden Smith was able to pay only about five shillings in the pound, but George Scrivens and Francis Smith assisted proceedings in every way and ultimately the bank's debts were paid in full. As a mark of public esteem for the manner in which he had acted, a silver candelabrum and an inkstand were presented to Scrivens in October 1858, and in the following year he was appointed manager of a newly opened Hastings branch of the Tunbridge Wells bank of Beeching & Sons, which was founded in 1815.[29]

The premises of the Old Bank were sold and, after some rebuilding, opened as a branch of the London and County Bank, which had first opened an office in Hastings in 1851. By 1863 this joint stock bank had 128 branches, most of them within the 65 mile radius of London. Seventeen of its offices were in Sussex, although some were sub-branches with restricted opening hours or days. At Pulborough a clerk travelled weekly from the Petworth branch to open an office at the Swan Inn on market days. By 1890 the Capital and Counties Bank, established in 1834, had seven offices in the county, two of them in Brighton, but it was not until 1890 that any major change took place in the structure of banking in Sussex.

In that year the firm of Beeching & Co. was taken over by Lloyds Bank Ltd., though Charles Beeching still remained as manager under the new regime. In December 1890 the death occurred of George Head, founder of the East Grinstead Bank, and the business passed to George Searle Head, his son and partner. Little more than a year later, on Thursday 24 February 1892 'intense excitement was aroused in the town and throughout the adjoining district . . by the suspension of payments at Messrs Head's bank. The bank premises were not opened at the usual time; but the following notice was exhibited on the door:

> Messrs G. and G.S. Head regret that they are compelled to suspend payment and beg to state that negotiations are being made with Lloyds Bank with the object of meeting the convenience of customers . .

The notice caused great consternation, as there are few tradesmen in the town who do not bank with Messrs Head who are also the custodians of the funds of the Literary and Scientific Institute, the Gas and Water Company, and the Local Board *(of Health)*. However the opening by Messrs Lloyds Bank of a sub-branch at Mr Marplesden's shop . . and another branch by the Capital and Counties Bank in the High Street . . tended to allay the fears of the townspeople'.[30]

Nevertheless, Head's debts amounted to some £162,802 and much of the bank's securities had already been transferred to the London and Westminster Bank, the London agents, who were themselves owed more than £50,000. They had on more than one occasion threatened to close the East Grinstead Bank since the death of Head's father when the bank had last been solvent. The failure was in fact caused by the bankruptcy of one of several local building contractors who had borrowed large sums to finance speculative housing and could repay no part of their debts. The builder, Francis Stevens, later admitted knowing for many months that he had been trading only at the mercy of the bank.

The failure aroused some anger, especially when it was revealed that large deposits had been accepted only the day before when it was known that failure was unavoidable, and 'a mob, numbering some five hundred persons, surrounded Brook House - the home of Mr Head, a mile or more out of East Grinstead westwards - trampling down the garden and at night giving "rough music". On one occasion Mr Head was escorted to his home under the protection of three policemen one of them mounted'.[31] Bankruptcy proceedings were lengthy and much complicated by the fact that the estate of George Head had not yet been discharged from Chancery and made available for distribution. Despite early confidence, only a limited payment was made to the impatient creditors, although immediately after the failure Lloyds Bank had offered depositors an advance of five shillings in the pound provided accounts were transferred to Lloyds.

This failure was an isolated event, however, for although the years 1892 to 1896 saw exceptionally low interest rates and 'cheap money' in the London markets, the provincial banks were better able to withstand the difficulties this caused. Outside of London the securities offered against loans were generally less sound; the bank's risk was greater but the competition for business was less and so higher interest rates could be charged. The London banking houses thus found it advantageous to extend quickly their provincial branch networks, either by opening new offices themselves or by amalgamating with established provincial banks. During the 1890s Lloyds Bank opened seven branches in Sussex, the London, City, and Midland Bank opened offices at Brighton and Eastbourne, while the London and South Western Bank and the London and Provincial Bank came to Brighton and Eastbourne respectively. At the same time the last of the old Sussex banks lost their independence.

In 1896 the Hentys sold what was still in essence a family business to the Capital and Counties Bank, bringing their total of Sussex offices to seventeen. This did not necessarily reflect any lack of faith by the Henty family in their banks. Like most private bankers they depended greatly on their personal reputations and so found difficulty in conducting business very far beyond where they were known and so could not compete with the services offered by the spreading branch networks of the joint stock banks. Capital for expansion was always in short supply, a problem that did not greatly trouble the joint stocks, while privately issued bank notes were becoming less acceptable to the public since the supply of gold coin and Bank of England notes was adequate. Coupled with the need to expand into the provinces to maintain their profitability, the joint stock banks were able to offer terms that were hard to refuse.

During the same year of 1896 there took place the greatest merger of banks then seen in England when fourteen banks joined with Barclay & Co. of Lombard Street. Eight of these were in the eastern counties, others in Darlington and Newcastle, Scarborough, Hertford and Huntingdon. In Sussex, Barclay & Co. took control of the Brighton Union Bank of Hall, Lloyd, Bevan & Co., and the Lewes Old Bank then operated by Messrs Molineux, Whitfeld, Whitfeld, and Molineux. These banks did not disappear entirely into the new organisation, for they remained as separate branch networks, and in the case of the Brighton bank, Messrs R.A. Bevan, B.Y. Bevan, and L.P. Bevan of the old firm were appointed as 'local directors' of Barclay & Co. to supervise its management.

A similar arrangement was made when in 1900 Barclay & Co. took over the Chichester Bank. The firm had seen the last of many reconstructions of the partnership in 1892 when it was reformed following the death of Charles Halstead, a Chichester ironmonger and iron founder. A new

Sussex bank offices I: The Lewes Old Bank, Lewes High St., which has been occupied by a bank since 1790, and below, Barclays modern branch office in Chapel Road, Worthing.

Sussex bank offices II: The Midland Bank, Terminus Road, Eastbourne, and below, National Westminster Bank, 86 Western Road, Brighton.

partnership was formed by the remaining members, Francis Gruggen and George Woodbridge, whose father, brother, and nephew were all in their times partners in Woodbridge, Lacy & Co. of the Uxbridge Old Bank. They were joined by Sir Peniston Milbanke of Eartham and James Gauntlet, and the capital of the new firm was £25,000. Milbanke died in 1899 and in the following year the business was sold to Barclay & Co. for 2,000 Barclay shares of £20 each, with £8 paid up on each. Barclay & Co. established a local head office at the East Street premises and Gruggen, Woodbridge, and Gauntlet were appointed local directors.[32]

Banking in Sussex developed with national trends into the twentieth century. In 1881 there had been 317 banks in England and Wales which operated a total of 2,382 branches. By 1891 the number of firms had dropped to 261, with 3,221 branches, and by 1901 only 172 banks remained although they maintained 4,872 offices.[33] During the 1900s, the National Provincial Bank, Parr's Bank, and the Union of London and Smith's Bank all opened branches within the county, and the already established banks opened new branches to serve a growing population. At the same time the total number of banking firms fell further to 199 by 1911, while the branch total rose to 6,413. This was the result of further absorbtion of small banks, but also of mergers between some of the large banking companies.

In 1909 the London and Westminster, oldest of the London joint stocks, joined with the London and County to form the London, County and Westminster Bank. A few years later a merger with Parr's Bank Ltd. led to the cumbersome name of the London, County, Westminster, and Parr's Bank which was soon shortened to the Westminster Bank. The National Provincial joined with the Union of London and Smith's Bank. In 1918 the

Capital and Counties Bank joined with Lloyds, so considerably increasing Lloyds' representation in Sussex, while the merger of the London Provincial and South Western with Barclays Bank Ltd., and a policy of opening many sub-branches had placed Barclays as the most numerous in the county.

By 1921 there were only 40 banking companies in England and Wales, but these had between them a total of more than 8,000 branch offices. This growth was spurred as more people made use of bank accounts, also as new offices were opened to serve suburban housing developments. The majority of these offices belonged to the newly emerged 'big five' of Barclays, Lloyds, the Midland, National Provincial, and Westminster, and growth was hastened as they developed truly national networks and competed to have a branch in every high street. Sussex was served by about 215 branches and sub-branches, of which only the 26 offices of the Midland Bank - the renamed London, City, and Midland Bank - had not been in some part acquired through amalgamations. By then the pattern of banking familiar today had been established, needing only the recent merger of National Provincial and Westminster banks to produce the current 'big four'.

This did not mark the end of competition, nor fix an immutable pattern on banking in Sussex or beyond. During the 1930s a vigorous campaign of expansion brought Martins Bank to Sussex, with new branches at Brighton, Hove, Eastbourne, and Bexhill, the last being closed for the duration of the war. Martins amalgamated with Barclays in 1969, but by then both the Trustee Savings Banks and the National Girobank had begun to offer new competition to the major joint stock banks. This has intensified with the growing diversity of alternative financial services, while the banks have themselves very greatly widened their range of business. However, the rising costs of maintaining an extensive network of branches and the trend toward automation suggest that the future of banking is likely to see at least as many changes as it has in the past two centuries.

Monogram of the Capital and Counties Bank

THE COUNTRY BANKS OF SUSSEX

Further information of changing partnerships and note issues may be found in:
G.L. Grant, *The Standard Catalogue of Provincial Banks and Banknotes*
(Spink & Son Ltd., London, 1977)

ARUNDEL BANK		
Bushby & Co.	c1790-1814	To Henty & Co.
Henty & Co.	1814-1896	To Capital & Counties.
ARUNDEL AGRICULTURAL BANK	1804-1813	Failed.
Olliver & Co.		
Arundel		Failed. To London
Hopkins, Drewett & Co.	1827-1841	& County Bank.
George Isaac Call & Co., Bognor	1824-1826	Failed.
BRIGHTON BANK	c1790-1793	Failed. Revived as
Harben & Co.		Brighton Old Bank.
BRIGHTON OLD BANK	1793-1826	Failed.
Mitchell, Mills & Co.		
SUSSEX COUNTY BANK, Brighton	1807-1826	Failed.
Tamplin, Gregory & Co.		

BRIGHTHELMSTON BANK Wigney & Co.	1814-1842	Failed.
BRIGHTON & SUSSEX BANK Lashmar & Muggeridge	1818-1825	Failed.
ROYAL BANK, Brighton John Kinnear	c1824	Failed.
CHICHESTER OLD BANK Ridge & Murray	c1785-1841	Failed. To London & County Bank.
CHICHESTER & SUSSEX BANK Diggins & Co.	c1788-1816	Failed.
CHICHESTER BANK Hack, Dendy & Co.	1809-1900	To Barclays.
EAST GRINSTEAD BANK John & Andrew Burt	1807-1816	Failed.
EAST GRINSTEAD BANK G. & G. S. Head	1842-1892	Failed. To Lloyds.
HASTINGS OLD BANK Tilden, Hilder, Harvey & Gill	1791-1857	Failed.
HASTINGS, HAILSHAM & TICEHURST UNION BANK Farncombe, Breeds & Co.	c1795-1825	Failed.

HORSHAM BANK		
Harben, Lanham & Co.	c1790–1793	Failed.
Grinsted & Lanham	1794–1816	Failed.
HORSHAM BANK	1809–1896	To Capital & Counties.
Henty & Co.		
SUSSEX & HORSHAM BANK	1810–1816	Failed.
Blunt & Raper		
Rickman & Son, Lewes	c1775–1790s	Gave up business.
LEWES OLD BANK	c1780–1793	Failed.
Harben & Co.		
LEWES OLD BANK	1789–1896	Founded as New Bank.
Molineux, Whitfeld & Co.		To Barclays.
LEWES BANK	1805–1825	Failed.
Wood, Hall & Co.		
John Stoveld & Co., Petworth	1806–1845	To London & County Bank.
RYE BANK	1790–1893	To Lloyds.
Curteis, Pomfret & Co.		
WORTHING & SUSSEX BANK	1809–1896	To Capital & Counties.
Henty & Co.		

Acknowledgements

This book is the result of research carried on over several years with help from many people. In particular I would like to thank:

The archivist and staff of the West Sussex County Record Office, Chichester.

The reference and local history librarians at Worthing and Chichester libraries.

Mr. John Norwood, curator of the Worthing Museum, for his assistance in photographing trade tokens. The museum holds an interesting collection of Sussex tokens which may be seen by appointment.

Mr. Alan Hill of Lewes, for generously allowing me to read his research on the growth of Martins Bank in Sussex, and assistance with the history of banks in Brighton and Lewes.

Mr. Alan F. Blanshard, the manager of the Lewes branch of Barclays Bank, successor to the Lewes Old Bank, for permission to examine some items relating to the Old Bank.

And for permission to reproduce illustrations:

West Sussex County Record Office.
West Sussex County Library Service.
Worthing Museum.
Barclays Bank PLC.
Punch magazine.

Bibliography

The foremost study in this field is Leslie S. Pressnell's *Country Banking in the Industrial Revolution* (Oxford U.P., 1956) which discusses in detail the business of the country banker.

Two books relate directly to private bankers of Sussex, most notably a biography of Thomas Dicker, the *Memorials of the Life and Times of a Late Country Banker*, a copy of which is in the local collection at Worthing library, and Marnie Basset's book on *The Hentys* (Oxford U.P., 1954) which chronicles the lives of Thomas Henty and his descendants in Australia.

Histories of individual banks include much information on banks they absorbed. Particularly useful are:

-A. Tuke, ed., *The History of Barclays Bank Ltd.* (London, 1927)
-W.F. Crick & J.F. Wadsworth, *A Hundred Years of Joint Stock Banking* (The Midland Bank) (London, 1936 & 1958)
-T.E. Gregory, *The Westminster Bank through a Century* (London, 1936)
-R.S. Sayers, *Lloyds Bank in the History of English Banking* (Oxford, 1957)

Kelly's directories provide an invaluable guide to the spread of branch networks, especially a network such as that of the Midland Bank which in Sussex grew by obtaining premises rather than absorbing local banks.

Trade tokens are more fully described in:

- R.C. Bell, *Commercial Coins, 1787-1804* (Corbitt & Hunter, Newcastle, 1963)
- R.C. Bell, *Commercial Copper Coins, 1811-1819* (Corbitt & Hunter, Newcastle, 1964)
- A.W. Walters, *Notes on the Silver Tokens of the Nineteenth Century* (Seaby, London, 1957)

NOTES

WSRO - West Sussex Record Office, Chichester

1 A.J. Taylor, 'Castle-building in Wales in the later thirteenth century' in *Studies in Building History*, ed. E.M. Pope (London, 1962) 104-133

2 I.W. Jones, *Money for All* (Llandudno, 1969) 12

3 E. Sykes, *Banking and Currency* (London, 1932) 87

4 W.F. Crick & J.F. Wadsworth, *A Hundred Years of Joint Stock Banking* (London, 1958) 13

5 I.W. Jones, 18

6 L. Pressnell, *Country Banking in the Industrial Revolution* (Oxford, 1956) 68

7 L. Pressnell, 299; *Sussex Archaeological Collections*, vol LXIV (1923) 79

8 *Sussex Weekly Advertiser*, 29 April 1793; WSRO Add Ms 26,355

9 *Sussex Notes and Queries*, vol 2, 255

10 Hastings Guide, 1794, 65

11 WSRO Add Ms 27,640

12 WSRO Add Ms 26,636/73

13 WSRO Add Ms 27,644

14 M. Basset, *The Hentys* (Oxford, 1954) 2-3

15 WSRO Add Ms 1,432

16 Rev G.P. Crawford, 'The Old Banks of Sussex' in *Sussex County Magazine*, vol 6 (1932) 252

17 M. Basset, 36, 440

18 WSRO Add Ms 1,005

19 WSRO MP 714

20 WSRO MP 1,175

21 *Sussex Weekly Advertiser*, 31 July 1815

22 Rev G.P. Crawford, 253

23 *Sussex Agricultural Express*, 27 Nov, 3 & 18 Dec 1841; 8 & 22 Jan, 19 & 26 Feb 1842
24 *Sussex Agricultural Express*, 30 April 1842
25 *Sussex Agricultural Express*, 12 March 1842
26 *Sussex Agricultural Express*, 23 April 1842
27 W.F. Crick & J.F. Wadsworth, 27
28 R.H. Mottram, *The Westminster Bank*, (London, 1936) 9
29 J.M. Baines, *Historic Hastings*, (Hastings, 1955) 249, 398
30 *West Sussex Gazette*, 3 March 1892
31 Rev G.P. Crawford, 252, quoting *East Grinstead Observer*